SIEGE OF POTCHEFSTROOM.

SIEGE
OF
POTCHEFSTROOM

COLONEL R. W. C. WINSLOE, C.B.

The Naval & Military Press Ltd

published in association with

**FIREPOWER
The Royal Artillery Museum**
Woolwich

Published by
The Naval & Military Press Ltd
Unit 10 Ridgewood Industrial Park,
Uckfield, East Sussex,
TN22 5QE England
Tel: +44 (0) 1825 749494
Fax: +44 (0) 1825 765701
www.naval-military-press.com

in association with

FIREPOWER
The Royal Artillery Museum, Woolwich
www.firepower.org.uk

The Naval & Military Press

MILITARY HISTORY AT YOUR FINGERTIPS

... a unique and expanding series of reference works

Working in collaboration with the foremost regiments and institutions, as well as acknowledged experts in their field, N&MP have assembled a formidable array of titles including technologically advanced CD-ROMs and facsimile reprints of impossible-to-find rarities.

In reprinting in facsimile from the original, any imperfections are inevitably reproduced and the quality may fall short of modern type and cartographic standards.

ILLUSTRATIONS.

Plan of the Gun Pits	Frontispiece.
Plan of Part of Interior of Fort	8
The Gaol at Potchefstroom	16
The Landroost's Office	24
Part of Interior of the Fort, Gaol in the distance ...	32
Part of the Interior of the Fort, after the evacuation. Magazine in the distance. Enemy's earthwork which commanded the Magazine is seen to the right of the buildings	40

PREFACE.

◆

IN an early number of *Macmillan's Magazine, 1883*, I wrote a short article giving a account of the investment of Potchefstroom Fort by the Boers during the rebellion in the Transvaal in 1880—81.

As so much attention has lately been given to South African affairs, I now venture to re-publish this article (slightly amplified and illustrated) in the hope that it may interest some of my old comrades, and such of the general public as may honour me with a perusal.

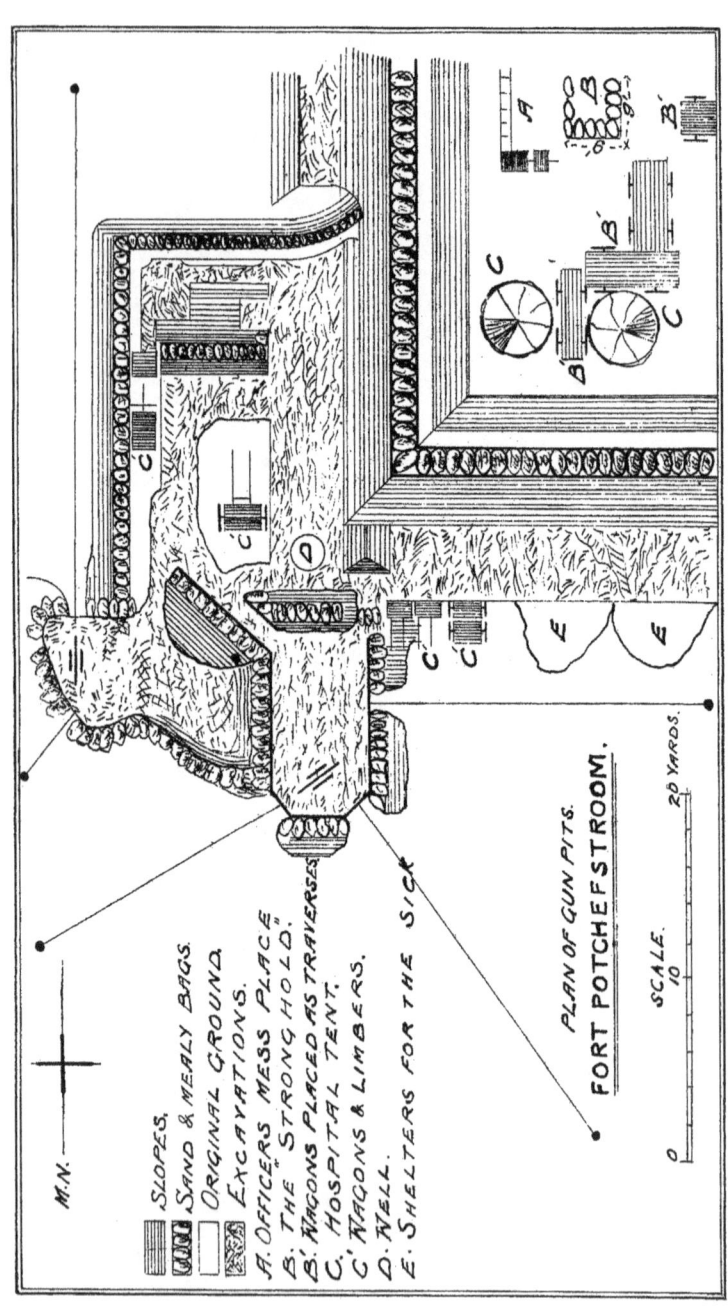

SIEGE OF POTCHEFSTROOM.

IN December, 1880, my regiment was quartered in Pretoria, the capital of the Transvaal and seat of Government; and at this time we were beginning to speculate on the probability of an early move towards the sea coast, to which officers and men were looking forward with a degree of pleasure only known to those who had done little else but march about from place to place since their arrival in the country, early in the year before.

Late in the afternoon of the 9th of December, 1880, in the course of my evening ride, I went into Government House, Pretoria, to pay a visit to Sir Owen Lanyon, the Administrator, when almost the first word his Excellency addressed to me, was, "Have you seen Bellairs?"

Colonel Bellairs, the late Sir William Bellairs, C.B., K.C.M.G., was then in command of the troops in the Transvaal.

I had not "seen Bellairs," but presently that Officer came forward, and I soon learned that I was to go to Potchefstroom at once, to relieve the Officer in command there, who, being Senior Officer of the Royal Artillery in South Africa, was required to join Head Quarters at Pretoria.

"When will you be ready?" was the first question. Now was the long-looked for opportunity come after many years of service, and I answered, readily enough, "Within a couple of hours if you wish it."

It was settled that I was to start the next day, and I set off at once to the Commissariat to make arrangements about a conveyance.

The Officers of my regiment were unanimous in congratulating me on my good fortune, for an independent command does not often come in the way of us soldiers, and when it does so is always duly appreciated.

It was known that there had been a dispute about the payment of taxes at Potchefstroom, or something of the sort, and there seemed at least a chance of a break in the monotony of life at Pretoria.

Next morning I left in a buck waggon, drawn by twelve mules, and did the distance, 110 miles, in forty-eight hours over a baddish road with several rivers to cross.

The first night I slept in my waggon (having "outspanned" to rest the animals); but the second was passed in my tent, which proved pleasanter in all ways."

That stirring events were on the *tapis* we had little idea; those in authority alone knew how affairs were progressing, and we soldiers were only anxious to obey orders and keep up the good name our regiment had won in the Zulu and Secocoeni campaigns. A Field Force, consisting of two guns of the N. Battery, 5th Brigade, Royal Artillery, twenty-five Mounted Infantry of the Royal Scots Fusiliers, two Companies of the same regiment, and a proportion of Commissariat and Medical Staff were already at Potchefstroom, under the command of Major Thornhill, Royal Artillery, and this I was destined to join, relieving the last-named officer. The strength of the force was 213 of all ranks, not including followers. The prevailing idea of the hospitable inhabitants I met on the road appeared to be wonderment that I had not been stopped *en route*, as many parties of armed Boers were at the time on their way to a meeting which was being held not far off. The place of this meeting was Paarde-Kraal—just about where Johannesberg now stands.

"So they let you go," said a man in a "Spider" (American Gig), "they" being an armed party that had just passed. I might have been outspanned at the time a bit off the road; for I never saw this party and I saw none along the road.

I arrived in Potchefstroom early in the afternoon of Sunday, the 12th December, 1880, and found that my coming was unexpected, and, of course, all hands were anxious to hear news from Pretoria. I was expected to be the bearer of important secrets of State, to be divulged without delay for the public benefit, and great was the disappointment when I had to confess that I knew as little as they did. My first thought was to look about me and see how the Camp was placed with regard to offence or defence, as the case might be. A fort, thirty yards square, had been commenced but had made little progress, and I saw that the water-furrow (channel) could not be long held with the force at hand; so we set to work at a well, which had been commenced, and also at the Fort which at this time was little more than a shelter trench. This was continued with little interval on the three following days.

The Fort afterwards, for purposes of defence, came to be reduced to about twenty-five yards square.

It should be understood that at this time I was indebted for advice to Major M. J. Clark, of the Royal Artillery, who had been sent to Potchefstroom by the Administrator as Special Commissioner.

During this time attempt was made to raise volunteers in the town, but with little success, owing to the unwillingness of the inhabitants, some of whom fearing to lose their Boer customers, and others having no sympathy with the British. Our Camp was pitched round the entrenchment; and the horses, mules, and oxen were in a small laager at some little distance.

After dinner we went down the town to the house of our kind friend the Consul-General for Portugal, the Chevalier Forssman.

This gentleman was a Member of the Legislative Assembly which sat at Pretoria, and there we had made the acquaintance of himself and family.

Friends dropped in, and there was much talk of the coming of the Boers and what was going to happen. The gentlemen were all of opinion that that there would be fighting ere long, but we placed no credit on this.

The ladies of the family sang to us, and we walked on the "Stoup," (a sort of verandah without roof,) in the moonlight and arranged to have a ball in two nights more in a vacant house close by. Our thoughts were, I am bound to say, a good deal directed as how we should amuse our fair friends at Potchefstroom; and all things promised well to our minds for a pleasant sojourn in the old capital of the Transvaal. The town covers a good deal of ground, most houses of the rich inhabitants standing in their own ground of about two hundred yards square.

These are mostly thickly studded with fruit trees, flowers are abundant, and hedges of cluster roses are everywhere to been seen in this, one of the most beautiful parts of the Transvaal.

On the 13th and 14th nothing unusual was observable in the town. We went about our ordinary millitary duties, and in the evening some of us again went to town, and spent some time with our friends, dancing and walking on the " stoup " by turns, while the voices of others could be heard singing inside.

On the 15th, my predecessor in the command was about to take his seat in the post cart *en route* to Pretoria, when he caught sight of the Boers entering the town, armed, and in force.

He was seen coming back to the Fort at full gallop, and we at once knew it was to warn us ; so in a very few minutes tents were struck, horses in the ditch, guns ready for action, and the parapet manned. Garrisons were sent to the Landroost's Office and to the Gaol, which places, previous to my arrıval, had been ordered by the Administrator to be occupied by the troops in case of necessity.

In the afternoon the family of the Consul-General for Portugal, the District Surgeon and his wife, and some others, sought refuge in the Camp. We had heard that the Boers had determined to take possession of their old capital on the 16th December, " Dingaan's Day," the anniversary of their victory over the Zulu King Dingaan ; and we now began to believe it. During the remainder of the day the Boers contented themselves with patrolling the streets, taking possession of the Printing Office, and stopping people who were about, and we thought that after issuing a proclamation they would leave the place. The military were not allowed to act in any way, so we remained in our lines getting things generally in order ; and luckily, as it turned out, we made good use of our time.

On the morning of the 16th our position was as follows :—The enemy held the town with its lines of walls, while we held the Fort, the Gaol, and the Landroost's Office. The guns were in shallow gun pits about two feet deep, at the north-east corner of the Fort facing the cemetery, which was distant about three hundred yards.

Between the Fort and the Gaol, a distance of three hundred and sixty yards, was open "veldt," sloping from the former to the latter, crossed by a water-furrow about one hundred and fifty yards from the fort.

Between the Gaol and the Landroost's Office, a distance of about four hundred yards, the space was intersected by walls and hedgerows, and the latter was by no means a nice place to retreat from. We all knew it was not an advisable place to occupy, but I felt bound by the orders of superior authority and there was no time for remonstrance.

The Gaol itself was a square building, with walls twenty feet high, standing in comparatively open ground.

The Landroost's Office was, on the contrary, surrounded by walls and houses with thatched roofs. In position therefore the enemy had every advantage.

The troops had still no authority to act, and we wondered what was to come next. About 9 a.m. we were breakfasting, with our guests sitting on the grass in little groups outside the Fort, tents struck, guns ready for action, Mounted Infantry horses saddled, and all ready for anything that might turn up, when a mounted party of about ten Boers, with their rifles at the "carry," came slowly riding past us at about one hundred and fifty yards distance, with the evident intention of surveying our proceedings.

This was going a bit too far ; so a few mounted infantry were sent to inform them that a patrol was not permitted so close to our camp, and to enquire their business. On seeing the Mounted Infantry approach, the Boers turned their horses and rode away at a trot. The Mounted Infantry followed as fast as the first road which enters the town, when they were fired upon from behind a wall close by. About a dozen shots were fired, when the Officer commanding the Mounted Infantry dismounted some of his men and returned the fire, with the result of severely wounding one of the enemy's patrol. The retire was immediately sounded, and we got within our entrenchment ; the two nine pounders were hastily surrounded with a few mealie sacks, and a few of the same were placed round the ditch to protect the horses. The ladies were protected in the same manner, and we waited the next turn in events.

We were not kept long in suspense, for shortly afterwards the Boers entered the Market Square in force and fired upon the Garrison of the Landroost's Office, which was situated in the Square.

The attack now became general; the enemy opening fire from the line of walls, and throwing out a right and left attack on our position. The head of the right attack got behind the walls of the cemetery, but was soon driven back by the fire of the two guns, and these also broke the advance of the main body which retired towards the north end of the town.

Quickly we went to work; and, with the Gaol, which was about half-way between the Fort and the Landroost's Office, were soon hotly engaged with the rebels who occupied the neighbouring houses and gardens. They came out well into the open and attacked the Fort; but our fire was apparently too much for them, and after about twenty minutes they retired repulsed on all sides, having lost a good number of men and horses. Cronjé, their leader, who we were afterwards informed had two horses killed under him, was afterwards well known to us as General Cronjé, Commanding the Burgher forces Potchefstroom Division.

Divided counsels evidently prevailed in the enemy's ranks, for had they attacked with anything like determination we should have had our work cut out for us. The guns being almost entirely in the open, had a specially bad time of it; but such soldiers as those of the N. 5, Royal Artillery to all appearance cared little for bullets, and only made an inward vow not to be made targets of again, if pick and spade could prevent it. The strength of the enemy on this occasion was about 800 mounted men; afterwards, on the 1st of January, their numbers increased to about 1,400, and towards the end, when reenforcements were sent to Laing's Neck, they never fell below 400. They were exceedingly well armed, generally with the best West Richards rifles (the favourite arm amongst the Boers); many had double express rifles, and a few carried explosive bullets, about the using of which protest was made without effect. One of our men had the flesh blown from his arm by one of these shells, and their explosions were frequently heard at night. During the greater part of this, the first day of active hostilities, heavy firing was going on throughout the position generally; and we worked all day and night, and for many nights after, in strengthening our defences. In the end the Fort became a really strong work, as indeed the searching and accurate character of the enemy's fire required it to be. On the night of the 16th, twenty-one women and children and five men came and asked for protection, and this was given them. Every night during the whole siege of ninety-five days we worked at the parapet, as the heavy rain often brought down the work of the day before. Sandbags got rotten, and the enemy's fire combined with this sometimes brought them down with a run, and we had to wait for dark before the damage could be repaired. This night work was very risky, as the enemy fired with wonderful accuracy in the dark, and they were able to come close to us without being observed as the grass stood always very high.

The mealies in our cattle lines had towards the end grown quite ten feet high, and this was inconvenient for us.

During the early part of the Siege, while the parapet was still low, moving about was anything but pleasant, and the Artillery were fully employed in clearing the enemy out of the trees with shrapnel, and from the house tops, where they never ceased to establish themselves. The busy inhabitants, during their leisure hours, would mount their house top occasionally for half an hours shooting at us, but they got a shell sometimes for their pains. One gentleman who was well known to us and his house carefully marked, had all his crockery smashed and some of his best drawing furniture destroyed—that taught him, and he retired from his dwelling during the remainder of our stay.

We had the pleasure of meeting him at dinner before we left Potchefstroom.

On the 17th firing was going on from all the positions most of the day. On the morning of the 18th communication which had been established with the Landroost's office by flag signal, was stopped, and we got no news of what was going on there. About 10 a.m., to the surprise of every one, the Union Jack was seen to be hauled down from the top of the Landroost's Office, and a white flag appeared in its place. Many were the speculations as to the cause—few guessed the real one; viz., that the officer in command had been forced to surrender.

A letter brought by a flag of truce informed us that the garrison had surrendered unconditionally to the enemy ; the position, never a good one, having become untenable.

We had learned before this by flag signal that Captain A. L. Falls of the Royal Scots Fusiliers, in command of the Landroost's Office, had been killed and some others wounded ; and we sympathised much with the officer left in command, that he had been compelled to give up the post that he had so well defended. We replied to this letter that the surrender of the Landroost's Office did not concern the other positions held by Her Majesty's Troops, and arranged for a truce until 4 p.m. for the carrying out of the retirement. During this time we worked liked fiends in strengthening our fort ; and well it was we did so, for shortly before the hour named the enemy opened a tremendous fire while the white flag was still flying, with the result of severely wounding one of our men at the Gaol. This act of treachery on the part of the enemy had no excuse, and had a bad effect on our men. It was now decided to abandon the Gaol, and the officer in command there received orders during the afternoon, by flag signal, to retire on the Fort on seeing a lantern on the parapet. This was shewn after dark, and the garrison retired noiselessly in skirmishing order, carrying their wounded on stretchers made with rifles. The Boers evidently did not anticipate this move, and it is strange that it was not observed, for the place was closely invested on three sides. The casualties at the Gaol were one man killed and two wounded.

We were glad to see our comrades back, as they had a bad time of it, and we knew the place could not have been held much longer. The upper walls were made of sun-dried bricks, through which bullets penetrated with ease ; and the lower loop holes could hardly be used with effect since the Boers fired with the greatest accuracy through them at short range. Our water supply now became a source of considerable anxiety.

We suffered greatly from want of water at this time, especially the private soldiers, who, being hard worked, required it most. Three pints a day, for all purposes, was the allowance ; and only those who have been reduced to this quantity can realize how little it is for men who were working hard day and night. As I said before we had commenced digging a well, and none of us will ever for-

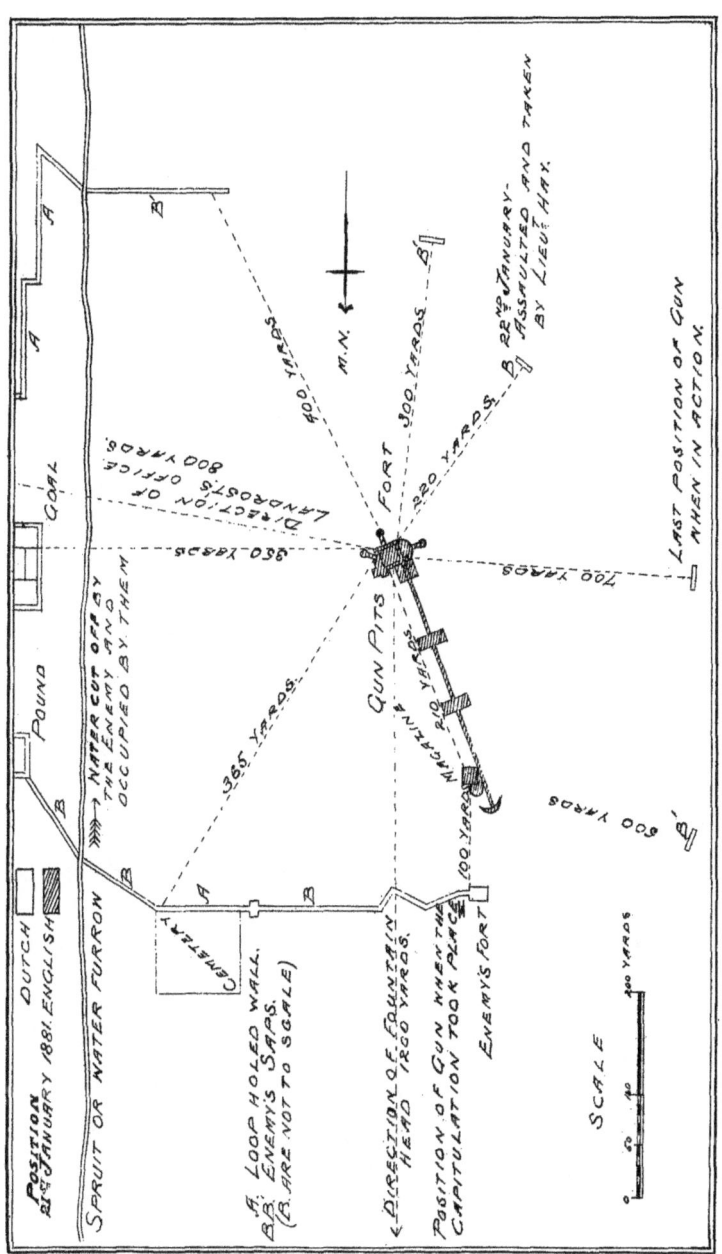

get how anxiously we watched the work as it progressed. We sunk tö a depth of thirty feet, sixteen of this through rock, and yet the yield was absolutely nothing—only a nine gallon cask each night and this more than half thick mud.

For three nights we managed to water our horses and mules, and fill our water carts, by sending them to the fountain head above the place where the water had been cut off a day or two before. Our procedure was something like the following :—The water carts started from the rear of the Fort after dark, attended by a small escort, the twenty-five Mounted Infantry and thirty soldiers went as a covering party, the remainder of the Garrison stood every man in his place on the parapet, and the Artillery at their guns. On the return of the water carts the horses went out, about one-third at a time. Some of the horses we watered at the water furrow before it was cut off, but on each occasion we lost some of them and had also men wounded.

It will be understood that at this time the place was not closely invested. It was an anxious time while these parties were away at a distance of 1,200 yards ; and as the operation had to be repeated several times, it took the greater part of the night. The rumblings of the water carts could be plainly heard by us on the parapet, and by the enemy also no doubt ; and it seemed strange to us that they did not sieze the water at the fountain head, which they could easily have done. It soon became apparent that this operation could be no longer performed, as the enemy were seen going in the direction of the water, and it became a question whether the horses and mules could be kept. On the 19th of December the animals had been without water for forty-eight hours, and the supply for the troops was nearly gone. Shortly after dark a storm came on, and sufficient water was caught to supply men and animals until the 21st. On this day the well still shewed no signs of yielding a sufficient supply, the horses and mules had been thirty-six hours without water, and evidently could not hold out much longer.

They were therefore turned adrift ; and, as they galloped off to the water, were caught by the enemy. There were seventy-six horses (nearly all of them magnificent black Australians) and one hundred and twenty-one mules. We kept a valuable mare, the property of

Lieutenant C. F. Lindsell of the Royal Scots Fusiliers, and she survived the whole of the siege, although twice wounded. This mare afterwards broke her back on the top of the Biggersberg when being thrown for the purpose of extracting a bullet received during the siege.

On the afternoon of the 21st it again rained heavily, and enough water was caught to last another three days. The original well still showed no signs of yielding, so I offered £25 to the first party of men who succeeded in finding water, and a number of squads of men started digging, one of which found water at a depth of fifteen feet. It filled to the top in no time, so we placed a barrel in it half filled with sand and charcoal and thus our greatest necessity was secured. The old well filled up with surface drainage, but was of no use for drinking purposes. I have dwelt thus long on the question of water as it was everything to us—on it depended our existence.

Very many of our horses and mules were killed, and it was a very painful sight to see the poor animals suffer.

Always at night we had to drag the carcasses to a distance, and this alone entailed great labour and loss on some occasions. On the 29th a flag of truce appeared, and the bearer handed to our messenger a printed paper containing a proclamation of the Transvaal Republic. On these occasions our messenger generally returned with a pipe in his mouth, and was the object of envy to everyone as we had nothing to smoke the whole time we were in the Fort. I always sent the same man, a sergeant, and he would always give his friends a bit on his return. A soldier does not often forget to share with a comrade; and the sergeant, being a favourite with the Boers, generally got some tobacco given him. He was one of my best men, an old Hibernian scholar, and from first to last exerted himself to the utmost in keeping the young hands in good humour—singing continually such songs as soldiers like, and particularly on the wettest and most unpromising days.

On the 1st January, at daylight the enemy commenced a fierce attack on our position, bringing into action a ship's gun throwing a ball of about 5 lbs. weight—and with this they pounded us merrily until silenced by our nine pounders. This we were able to do at first; but later on they used to surround their gun with woolsacks or sandbags, and roof it in and so made it difficult to silence.

Having immense command of labour, they were able to do anything they chose. The fire on this morning was terrific, and delivered from loopholed walls, trees, and house-tops; so that it could only be silenced in detail by Artillery fire.

The garrison kept under cover for upwards of an hour and a half. While this was going on every man sat at his post, rifle in hand, singing part songs to while away the time, while the ladies joined in the refrain. The buglers assisted in this; and the men were much amused at the vigour of the enemy, while we replied not a shot, waiting for the rush at the Fort, which was every moment looked for. When the commotion ceased our time came; and we " let them have it " as they went home to breakfast, but the uselessness of this soon became apparent, so we sounded the breakfast bugle and the duel came to an end. One thing was particularly noticeable during the Siège, and that was that the Boers have a great regard for themselves and never allowed us a good look at them the whole time.

They could have taken the Fort over and over again at any time by day or night—it would have been uncomfortable to try, but they could have done it easily.

Our loss on this occasion was not great, but every now and then one of our comrades fell, shot through a chink in the sandbags. The loss of one of our number was, in truth, only to be compared to that of a personal friend.

I venture to say that on few occasions in the history of the British Army have officers and men been more closely associated than during this Siege; officers came to know their men, men came to know their officers, and each learned to put their trust in the other and to work together. A good feeling was observable always and we thought ourselves hard to beat; which I hope we would have been if the Boers had ever ventured to rush the Fort.

As I said before this would have been an easy task, for the grass stood the height of a field of corn all round us, and they could have come very near without being seen. Many times we tried all we knew to burn it, but without effect, as it was green the whole time. Cronjé told me afterwards that, had he known what the Fort was like, he would have stormed it. The truth of the matter is that the Fort was very much stronger than he thought it was, as we worked day and night the whole time in making it so. Numbers of course would have done it and that he had. The plan we were told afterwards was to get 2,000 Caffres to come straight at us, and then the Boers were to come on when we were exhausted, or very few of us left. It would have been a cowardly thing to do, but I was told this myself in Potchefstroom.

At that time the Caffre Chiefs were too loyal to fight against us ; now we cannot say as we have left them to the mercy of harder taskmasters. One Caffre Chief sent to me to say he was coming with 3,000 men to relieve me, but his letter only reached me after the capitulation. This Chief was lately in England and I wish I could have shaken him by the hand.

It may be interesting to learn something of our daily routine of duty. At about 7 a.m. all breakfasted ; we in our little mess place, the men sitting about anywhere, that they could find room ; then the *terre-plein* of the Fort was swept, or scraped with spades in wet weather, and the drainage of the place looked to.

On a report being made, I went round and had a general look at affairs ; the work executed by the enemy during the night was discussed, and our work for the day settled upon. This, of course, greatly depended on what the rebels had been doing during the night, as we were pretty nearly surrounded by their works and they were continually at something new. The doctor attended to the sick and wounded, and the commissariat officer went about his duties. Previously to this every man stood his rifle and ammunition against his place on the parapet, and then the men off duty were generally free to look after their own affairs. All then soon settled down into general quietness, unless anything happened to prevent it, which was too often the case. A certain number of men were told off daily to keep down the fire of the enemy, and they soon acquired great accuracy of shooting, the ranges having all been taken previously to the investment. About 5 p.m. the guards mounted, and night sentries were placed after dark, after which not a word was spoken above a whisper or a light allowed, except on very urgent occasions when required by the doctor.

Once an amputation had to be performed at night, and the scene will not easily be forgotten by those who witnessed it. It was pitch dark, and silence reigned as usual in our little community when the doctor began his share of the night's work, which of course required a light. This made visible to the enemy the upper part of the tent, and as a matter of course, they directed their fire on it. The operation to be performed was the taking off an arm above the elbow.

Bullets were whizzing through the tent top while the patient, who by the way was my servant, lay on the amputating table; and the operation was successfully performed under chloroform, strange to say, without anyone being hit. Glad we were when the man recovered, for he was a great favourite. He is now a pensioner, and I hope honoured in his native town as he should be, for he is a very gallant young fellow, having sent in his name every time volunteers were called for during the Siege. His wound occurred while he was holding a basin for me to wash my hands before dinner when a bullet struck him between the wrist and the elbow. As it was a nasty wound he was put to lie down in the hospital tent and while there a round shot came and shattered his elbow.

The operation had to be put off until night, as our doctor wished for the assistance of the District Surgeon (one of our refugees) who at that time lived in the Magazine, and it was not advisable to risk valuable lives by coming across in the daytime unless in case of necessity, the sap at this time having become risky to say the least of it.

One of our chief industries was the making of sandbags, in the manufacture of which we cut up every tent, and indeed everything else that was possible to convert to such use. The wounded and convalescents were chiefly employed in this word, and they were presided over by an Irish sergeant, who was indefatigable in providing these, one of our principal requirements. Many thousands of bags were made, but we were sometimes at our wit's end to know how to get enough of them. I never entered into the subject of how they were to be made, but just ordered a certain number to be ready by night, and there they were in rows ready to be counted as sure as the night came. It reminded us of counting the game after a *battue*, but was much more interesting,

About an hour before dark we dined; and we would then sit for a while discussing our day's work and often talking of the army that was coming to relieve us and scatter the Boers to the four winds. Alas, this was destined never to come off, but lucky it was for us that we firmly believed it always, until the end, when we were roughly and suddenly undeceived. Soon after the ladies would get up to retire, and then there was saying goodnight—often unnecessarily prolonged, I believe, and as an Irish member of our company used to say, " in perfect silence."

If any of my readers happen to be of the fair sex they will understand how much assistance would be required in getting through a hole about two feet by one and a half; and I believe some of the younger members of our flock were impressed with the belief that our charges were suffering from lameness from the amount of care with which they helped them into the "Stronghold," as the soldiers named their apartment.

To have gone over the top of this would have been highly dangerous, as bullets struck the topmost bags continually. The ulsters of the ladies showed many bullet holes from having been left on the top of the "Stronghold " which was only five feet high.

On dark nights a few sentries were placed in pits dug for the purpose, and sandbags were placed round to make the shelter better. The pits were approached by small zig-zag trenches; but on moonlight nights these outlying sentries were withdrawn, and we trusted to those on the parapet. At guard mounting the officers for night watch were told off for two hours' duty at a time. These officers always remained in the centre of the Fort (there was a chair of state for the officer on duty, and the ground for the orderly bugler) and had sole charge of the ship for the time being; all others slept peacefully except the sentries, while the enemy kept up a pretty steady fire all night.

The writer of this kept watch from 2 to 4 a.m. (other officers by roster), and at the latter hours, and sometimes earlier, we all fell into our places and remained there until daylight, when all went to sleep again until 6.30 a.m. The cooks lit their fires at daylight and prepared breakfast.

A party was told off nightly to work at the parapet, Lieutentant K. E. Lean had always charge of this and in it he took the greatest interest. As I mentioned before the fire from the town was wonderfully accurate during

SIEGE OF POTCHEFSTROOM. 15

the night, and there was always too much of it to make exposure on the parapet pleasant. At night also the native drivers and leaders baled the water out of the ditch, as this on two sides could never be drained, and the stench was now and then indescribably awful. But, luckily, as I take it, the wonderful climate we were in, and the fresh open air life we led, neutralised the effect of this poison, and we suffered I think less from this than might have been expected. We were a very merry and happy party, all hands working willingly and cheerfully to one end, and no doubt this too had its effect.

Most of us were very sick, however, and for long times; but still all did their work, though hardly able to walk and troubled as little as possible our kind doctor, who himself was not always as fit as he might be. Now and then thoughts of home and of the loved ones there would come over us, and we knew that our case was better than theirs; but such-like thoughts were so often rudely dispelled by the work in hand that they seldom lasted long. Occasionally we had an artillery duel in the middle of the night, and then would come the musketry until both sides were tired with this interruption of their repose. Once, and once only, was the alarm sounded without cause during the night, and on this occasion every man was in his place on the parapet before the bugle had finished sounding. The men were then told that this would not be done again for practice, and praise for their smartness in turning out was not withheld. Every man slept with his rifle and ammunition at his right hand, and each night the officer on duty went round to see this order complied with.

On the night of the 3rd January we occupied a small magazine as an outpost, and held it until the end of the Siege. It was situated two hundred yards from the Fort and in a good position for adding to our defence, and the enemy never relaxed in their endeavours to take it, having, at the last, succeeded in sapping up to within eighty yards of the building, and erecting there a large and well constructed work which completely commanded it, and on which our Artillery had no effect. Many a time they pounded this magazine with their gun, and pierced the wall and roof, so we built an earthwork communicating with it, into which the garrison went when necessary. Lieutenant C. F. Lindsell of the Royal Scots Fusiliers was commander of this outpost, and he had with him twenty picked men of the Mounted Infantry—a more determined lot it would be hard to find. The place was by no means a bed of roses, but my mind was easy while they were there as I knew my men.

The enemy, having practically unlimited command of labour, sapped round us in all directions, keeping us fully employed in defilading our works.

This question of defilade was throughout a troublesome one, involving much labour to the garrison. We had seventeen mule and ox waggons, but these were standing outside the Fort—many of them at a distance. We determined to make use of some of them as traverses, and admirably they answered the purpose, for they enabled us to man our parapet without anything like the loss we should have had without them, and also made moving about more agreeable. The difficulty was to get hold of them, and this was accomplished by sending out a man at night to creep up to a waggon and attach a chain to it—then, by adding chains until they reached the ditch, we dragged the waggon close and took it to pieces at our leisure, bringing it inside, and finally placed them in a zig-zag fashion across the Fort. The waggons were then filled with earth as high as it would stand and finished off with sandgags tightly lashed in their place.

The Fort contained 322 men, women, and children, and was only twenty-five yards square inside We had also inside five ox waggons placed as traverses, five bell tents for sick, one for surgery, one hospital marquee for Commissariat Stores, one ammunition cart, and last of all the "Stronghold;" so it will seem we were very closely packed.

Our ladies, as we called them were a great care to us. Suffice it to say, their behaviour in danger and privation was admirable, and not to be surpassed. Never could I have believed that tender women could have done as they did. They came into the Fort with only what they stood in, and of course, suffered unheard of hardships. A shelter of mealie sacks about nine feet square and five feet in height had been made for them, in which was a small hole at the bottom to creep through; and in this they lived for upwards of three months, never coming out without permission being first obtained, and then only into a small shelter adjoining, in which we had our meals.

THE GAOL AT POTCHEFSTROOM.

Here we were comparatively safe from bullets, although they occasionally came in ; but, when the rebels got their gun to work in the rear of our position and tock our front parapet in reverse, we had to take down the "Stronghold," and I began to wonder what next to do for the safety of our charges. The sacks would have been no protection against round shot ; and so, when the gun was in action, we placed the ladies in a dug-out hole, and at night (when it seldom fired), they slept in a tent. This tent was riddled with bullet holes—there was not an inch square in any of the tents without a bullet hole—and so they got terribly wet and this was the case everywhere. The "Stronghold" had a waggon sail roof propped up by a couple of tent poles ; but this soon got so full of bullet holes that, when it rained, the water entered in torrents and drenched everything within. When this happened at night, the occupants had to get up and huddle into a corner, cover themselves with a bit of canvas to keep their clothes dry, and so wait for daylight.

It happened that we were on the skyline, and, consequently, visible on all but the very darkest nights ; so all night long the bullets would tear through the roof of the ladies' lodging, sending, often, splinters of the tent pole over them, but never a word was said. They seemed always to have the most perfect confidence in their defenders.

The blow came at last, however. One died, a young wife stricken with typhoid fever, and things wore a different aspect in the Fort that day. All, to the youngest drummer, were sorrowful ; rough men seemed subdued at the loss of this bright young face from our midst. We signalled to the enemy and asked that a coffin might be made in the town, and next morning one came filled with most lovely flowers ; these were the gift of relatives who obtained permission of the authorities to send them. Some wreaths of stephanotis and other flowers were there also, and these we placed on the coffin before lowering it into the grave. A black dress for the mother, and some ribbons of the same colour for the sisters were thrown aside by our antagonists—why we never could tell as they could not have done harm to anyone. The interment took place immediately, in full view of the enemy, a truce for one hour having been arranged for the purpose.

Our watches were not in the best order perhaps, or

probably none of us looked at them ; for while filling in the grave a round shot reminded us that time was up. We were inside our entrenchment quickly enough and and our guns in action, forgetting for a moment the work on which we had been engaged. Thus it was with us always—thought was set aside, and it was well that it was so. So ended one of the saddest incidents of the Siege.

Once only was one of the ladies wounded, and this happened towards the end when want of exercise was telling sadly on them. Our doctor had been continually impressing on me the necessity of their taking exercise ; and so, after much solicitation and also much doubt as to the result, I gave them leave to walk about the Fort with their father one afternoon when there was less firing than usual. Hardly had they gone out of our mess place when I heard a scream at my elbow, and there was one of the youngest girls lying on the ground. I thought she was killed ; but on examination the wound proved slight, and in a few days it healed. The bullet struck her at the back of the neck, and just missed the spine. After this the wish for a constitutional was not so general.

On the 7th January we had a night adventure. The enemy had been working hard for some nights behind the cemetery wall, 360 yards distant, and we wished to find out what they were after. Volunteers, as usual, were plentiful. An officer, and six men were chosen to go and have a look at the Boers at close quarters, and a hazardous business we all knew it was likely to be. The Cemetery is a large enclosure, some 300 yards square or more ; and we knew it was always occupied at night behind the walls on the near side, and on the far side was a large covering party.

The night was pitch dark and perfectly still when the small party set off by a circuitous route on their voyage of discovery, and we in the Fort stood every man ready to cover the retirement of our comrades. They were a long time getting there, and we were beginning to wonder what had become of them, when suddenly we heard our men fire a volley, and then came the sound of a revolver, and then two more volleys. Then there was a considerable commtoion, in which we joined, for we knew our party were retiring, and it was long before we were on anything like friendly terms again, for I believe the enemy thought we were most of us out there. They certainly showed that they had no lack of ammunition, and it was pretty hot for a time. In the midst of it all our party returned unhurt. They had crept up to the wall unseen, and at five yards distance had fired three volleys into the enemy, who were working at a trench with their rifles lying near, and we suppose they could not find them in the dark. The situation was not altogether an enviable one for the Boers, and we guessed that they would keep a better look out for the future.

On the 16th January a letter reached us by a flag of truce from the husband of one of our lady refugees, who had managed to get into the town from his farm in the country, and the lady was allowed to leave and join her husband. Later on this was not allowed; for towards the end of the siege I asked for the ladies to be allowed to leave and it was refused, as they knew we were short of provisions. Such is war sometimes, but the fact was that our enemy was content to starve us out. I was one of those who always said they would never attempt to storm the Fort, and it turned out that I was right. Numbers, of course, would have done it easily, and many of us wondered that the attempt was never made after the first day.

During this truce, which, as usual, only lasted a few minutes, a discharged German soldier jumped up on the top of the Boer trench, called out to ask how I was getting on, hoping I was unwounded, &c. And said, "Tell the Colonel you would never have held out so long if he had not been a German." Well, I am not a German, but the man took me for one of my brothers, with whom he had served in the army of the Fatherland.

By the messenger, who carried the flag of truce, came a letter in telegraphic cipher, purporting to come from Colonel Bellairs, commanding the troops in the Transvaal, informing me that he had come to our relief, and would be with us the next morning. We were to go out next morning and a great fight was to take place, and the Boers were to be driven away. The trick was a clumsy one, and we paid no attention to it. The signal failed, or we never saw it; but, sure enough, next morning, in a drenching rain, we heard heavy firing in a wood about a mile off, and the cannon was also heard. The enemy got their morning's amusement for nothing; and they must have had some trouble in drying themselves, for the rain could not well have been heavier. We saw them coming home, many of them got up in red coats for our benefit, so we gave them a shell or two to quicken their movements. This precious document, I was afterwards told, was concocted at Heidelberg, and it did little credit to its author.

On the 22nd of January, a trench which the enemy had opened 220 yards in our rear, threatened to become troublesome, so I determined to take it. Volunteers were called for, and I selected Lieutenant Dalrymple Hay, one sergeant, and ten men for the storming party. They went out in the most dashing manner in broad daylight across the open veldt. Three men fell before they had left the Fort a few yards, and one of these died of his wound a few days later.

There were eighteen of the enemy in the trench, three of whom escaped. Four were taken prisoners, and we saw eleven fall as they were running away. Our party were under a tremendous cross fire while charging this trench, and this we kept down as much as possible with every rifle we could muster. We succeeded in exchanging the four Boers for four of our own men, who had been taken prisoners at the Landroost's Office, on December 18th. Directly our party got back a man appeared carrying a huge Geneva Cross flag, and this proved to be a doctor who was sent to attend the wounded. We hoisted the white flag, and he came up, looking anything but happy, as he had been in fear of his life all the way out lest we might fire on him. We sat down under a waggon outside the Fort, and had a pleasant chat, while our doctor attended to the wounded. The Boer physician was an old acquaintance, we having known him formerly at Standerton as a photographer, and from this place he told us he had been summoned to Potchefstroom to attend the Burghers there. He had much faith in our doctor it was evident, for he never troubled himself with his wounded men, but sat and talked with us. He presented me with a handsome carved pipe, and I had my first smoke for over a month. For this, and perhaps other delinquinces, we afterwards heard, he was put in irons by the Boer commander. On coming out of the Fort two months later he showed us his hand minus a finger, which loss had occurred from our fire, and we were sorry for this for he was there against his will and was not fighting against us. We lent the enemy stretchers to take away their wounded, and next morning they were returned with fruit for our wounded, and also some carbolic acid which our doctor had asked for. We thanked the Boer commander by letter, and so this affair ended.

Civilities like this take the sting off warfare, and I must say for the Boers that they were never behind hand in such things. They are a fine, manly, sturdy race, such as I should like to live among. Who can blame them for fighting for their independence ? We, at least, never did so.

About this time we began to think of the coming of a relief column. Each made his calculations as to the probable time of its arrival ; and, need I say, these widely differed ? There was one point on which we all agreed, and that was in our trust and belief in Sir George Pomeroy Colley, who we knew would strain every nerve to reach us. There was something about Sir George that inspired soldiers, and those of us who knew him had caught the contagion. His was a courteous, soldierly manner that would have gone a long way with a people like the Boers. Great was our grief when afterwards we heard of the death of this distinguished officer ; and such of us as had dear ones at home did not forget to think of those he had left, and who had, to temper their grief, only the remembrance of how nobly he fell.

A look out party had been organised under an officer. All the hill tops within view were watched day and night for signals, and the best measures at our disposal were taken for answering any that might be made. A heliograph was constructed out of a looking glass, and kept always ready. One night, just as I was turning in, a look-out man called me. Rockets were seen on the top of the Swartz Kop, and the relieving force was on the road and would be with us in two days. All turned out to see the welcome sight—ladies in their Ulsters, and wounded from their beds ; but they had better have slept. These signals certainly looked liked rockets and for a time we were deceived.

Some of us dreamt that night that they heard the bagpipes coming down the Heidelberg road to the tune of "The Campbell's are coming." Next morning looking over the parapet was as hazardous as ever, and a helmet on the top of a bayonet soon reminded us that "discretion is the better part of valour." For us such disappointment as this did not signify, but for our wounded soldiers it was different. They could only lie on their beds and wonder who would be the next to join them. Our wounded did very well until the last ten days or so, when every man who got a wound died. The place became so unhealthy that gangrene set in at once and there was no hope for anyone. My servant was the last man that recovered.

On the 23rd of January about thirty of the mule and ox drivers left the Fort at night by their own desire, and we were glad of this relief to our commissariat. Some of these poor fellows were shot by the Boers in escaping, and a very few came back unable to get away.

On the 4th of February, a flag of truce brought us a copy of the *Staats Courant* (Transvaal Government Gazette) of the 2nd of February, containing an account of the action fought near the Ingogo by the troops under the command of Sir George Colley, and this did not tend to raise hopes of immediate relief. This was, of course, sent to discourage us by our adversaries, who at this time no doubt expected our capitulation daily. We sent by the bearer a message to the Boer Commander to the effect that we should be pleased to receive the paper regularly, but I am afraid he must have thought we were poking fun at him. On these occasions the Boers did not allow their messenger to remain longer than a few seconds—just time to hand in the letter and go away.

Our sergeant, who was a good deal of a wag, generally managed however to have a word or two, when something like the following would pass:—

Boer—"When are you coming out?"

Sergeant—"Oh, never! we like it so much. We have plenty to eat and drink. When are you coming to take the Fort?"

Boer—"When our best men come we are going to rush the Fort. General Colley is not coming."

Sergeant—"Goodbye. Thanks for the tobacco,"

Boer—"Goodbye."

He would come back looking the picture of good humour, and the soldiers would gather round to hear the latest from the town. He would sit down and gather a lot of men round him and tell them marvellous tales, all invented for the occasion but serving to amuse, and that was what was wanted.

All the garrison were in the open the whole of the time, and this was very trying, as it was the rainy season —this and the hot weather come together in this part of Africa. The bell tents were dug out for a depth of about eighteen inches, and in one of these a round shot smashed the thigh of one of our poor fellows, who was lying wounded, and shattered the arm of another. The latter was the man the amputation of whose arm I described before. I mention this to show how the round shot found its way into apparently impossible places. The tents at the last were not enough for the sick, and it was necessary to put infectious cases elsewhere.

To accomplish this we had to dig holes in the outside wall of the ditch, and there put the worst cases. A brother of one of the ladies died of typhoid fever in one of these holes, and it was a sad sight to see one of the sisters sitting day and night there, watching her sick brother. We did all we could for them, and that was little enough.

After the first few Sundays, at least during the day time, little shooting went on, and by mutual consent we left each other alone. I always read the Church of England Service to our little mess, while Captains read Morning Prayer to their men on the parapet. Our Commissariat Officer, who had been one of the brave defenders of Rorke's Drift, read the Roman Catholic Service to men of that Church. That we had a few sympathisers in the town was evident; for on Sunday afternoons we several times saw a whole family come out from behind a wall and wave handkerchiefs to us; and this we took to be a friendly greeting, as no doubt it was. We could hear the singing in the Dutch Churches in the town on Sundays; and in the trenches the Boers used to collect on Sunday nights and sing Psalms for an hour or so, sure of being undisturbed, as they always were.

We sent away a number of letters during our captivity, but to only one did we receive an answer. This was a letter I sent to the Officer Commanding in the Transvaal, on the 16th December, and to which I received an answer about six weeks afterwards—in this we were informed of the disaster to the 94th at Bronkir's Spruit. Also I sent a few letters to *The Times* newspaper, and to my home in Scotland, none of which reached their destination. They were all done up in a quill, and should have escaped detection. They were taken out by Caffres who crept out after dark; and, with the exceptions of one who I know was caught and his message read, we never heard what became of them. Twice only did a European succeed in getting away; on the first occasion he returned half starved, having been unable to cross the Vaal, twelve miles off; and on the second occasion two brothers, Nelson, succeeded in reaching the Head Quarters of Sir Evelyn Wood, at Newcastle, in Natal. These gentlemen swam the Vaal near De Wit's Drift, and reached Newcastle through the Orange Free State, by way of Kronstadt and Harrismith. We knew nothing the whole time of what was going on outside, and often wondered what our friends would think of our silence. On reaching Ladysmith, on the 2nd of May, we found two sacks full of letters awaiting us. I, myself, received thirteen letters from my home in the North, not to mention many others.

For food we were badly off the whole of the time. All our cattle were lost on the 17th of December, and we had no fresh meat the whole time, except nine cows, which we captured during the first few days; and we were so closely invested that not an ounce of food got into the Fort during the siege. On Christmas Day we intended having roast horse instead of roast beef for dinner; but it turned bad, and at the last moment had to be rejected by our *chef*, and we contented ourselves with something less succulent. We went on reduced rations on the 19th December (the fourth day of the siege), and further reductions were made from time to time.

On the 11th of January we began to issue half-a-pound of mealies (Indian corn) three times a week in lieu of the same quantity of biscuits, and on the 22nd of January this was made a daily issue. These mealies were the food of the horses and mules. On the 15th of March we were reduced to one pound of mealies and half-a-pound of Caffre corn (millet) daily, with a quarter of a pound of preserved meat on alternate days, and nothing else whatever.

Tea, coffee, sugar, salt, rice, biscuits, and indeed everything else was exhausted long before. All were weak from having to work hard on this kind of food, but health was fairly maintained notwithstanding. The mealies and

THE LANDROOST'S OFFICE.

Caffre corn were pounded by the men, and when boiled proved wholesome and comparatively nuitritious. The husk, however, was only partially got rid of, and this made us all ill.

We baked excellent bread for the sick from a small store of flour ; but no one else got any, except the ladies who got a small quantity, and this gave out some time before the evacuation.

The bread was baked in a hole in the parapet, and no better oven could be found. Dysentery and diarrhœa were always prevalent, and none escaped one or the other. Towards the end there was a good deal of enteric fever, and a few cases of scurvy.

When our beef tea was finished, we made a substitue from preserved Australian beef, but it gave little nourishment. To keep off scurvy the men were ordered to boil grass and young mealie stalks in their food, and this was undoubtedly very beneficial.

Our wood came to an end on the 15th of January, and we then began burning our waggons, and but for this we should have been in a bad way. We burnt the whole of the waggons except five, which were used for traverses inside the Fort, but were able to keep the ambulance waggons, water carts, and ammunition carts.

These would have gone had we remained much longer. The Boers were entitled to keep the ambulance ; but, as we wanted it for our sick, they lent it to us and we returned it after passing through the Orange Free State. I have always felt much indebted to the Boer Commander for his courtesy to us ; and really nothing could exceed the pleasant manner in which everything was condncted with the Boer leaders during our brief stay at Potchefstroom after the capitulation.

All tents, tarpaulins, and everything else that we could lay hands upon was cut up to make sand bags; a few pieces only being reserved to cover ourselves on rainy nights. With this exception, all hands were in the open, day and night during our time in the Fort, and this was the rainy as well as the hot season. After the first few days we had no tobacco, and many men smoked tea leaves, coffee grounds, and mealie leaves.

A smoking mixture composed of the two first named was quite the rage at one time. Soon, however, it got out of favour, and we contented ourselves by looking at our pipes occasionally, and seeing that they were ready for action when the time came. We had a few gallons of rum, which was served out in wet weather on five or six occasions; but our drink was water, of which we had plenty when our well got into working order.

On the 20th of March we had only the following left; nothing else, of any kind that was eatable being in the place:—

Mealies (whole)...	1,600lbs.	All damaged, however, having been three months in the parapet.
Kaffir corn (whole)	5,006	
Preserved meat	24lbs. ...	This had been reserved for the sick.
Rice ...	16lbs. ...	
Erbswurst, 40 rations	...	

The silence at night, coming as it did soon after dark, was often irksome, especially as we had not much in the shape of diversion. One of my officers, a lieutenant of artillery, seemed to feel this unaccustomed quietude, for he would come to me sometimes and say, "Would you allow me just to give a screech?" "Yes," I would say, "but first tell the sentries, or they might take a fancy to shooting you." This done, he would get up on the top of the parapet and commence a series of most unearthly yells. The Boers, not understanding this performance, would promptly open fire while we lay low and amused ourselves by listening to the commotion. He was down from the parapet in a moment, and feeling all the better for the exertion. Occasionally, the men would put a lantern on the top of a pole at night, and this always raised a commotion in the enemy's lines, for they would fire incessantly. At night we communicated with the Magazine by lanterns, and very useful this kind of signalling was found.

Amongst our many requirements was a Union Jack. One was made in the Gun Pits by men of the Royal Artillery; they were allowed to retain it, and it was in possession of the N. Battery, 5th Brigade, Royal Artillery, until the Battery was broken up some years ago. It was made from coat linings, and has a good number of bullet holes to show. It displayed its folds for exactly two months on our parapet, a visible sign that the little garrison had some life left, and could still do something for the honour of their Queen and of the army to which they were proud to belong. A few years ago the N. Batt. 5th Brigade, Royal Artillery, was marching somewhere near Windsor, when the Queen took the opportunity of inspecting it ; and a few days after, I am proud to say, Her Most Gracious Majesty was pleased to inspect the flag at Windsor Castle.

After dark, on the 8th of March, I was informed that a Dutchman had been captured, and that he wished to see me. I was taken to a lonely part of our Magazine Sap, and there sure enough was our friend , or rather spy, as I took him to be, and have always thought him. We were left alone in the darkness, and the man began his tale, of which I could make nothing, as he trembled so that he could hardly speak.

Perhaps he had heard of the ferocity of the " Rooi Badges," or " Red Coats," as the Boers called us ; and expected nothing better than instant annihilation. I thought we were quite alone, but found that one of my officers deemed that a little company might be desirable ; for, thinking I heard a movement behind me, I looked round, and there was the sentry, with his bayonet within an inch of the back of the man's neck. This finished matters, for he could not speak at all now ; so thinking, I suppose, that deeds were better than words, he stood up and to my astonishment discovered to me that he was tobacco all over, literally from head to foot. The tobacco was made up like a rope, about an inch in diameter, and was wound about his body, and his pockets also were stuffed with the same. The sentry dropped his rifle now, and we two unrolled the Dutchman, making him turn round until he was giddy, and in less than no time we were weighing the precious weed into portions and distributing it all round. By way of reward for this thought of our wants, we handcuffed him there and then, and chained him to the wheel of a waggon for the night, and so he remained always, except in the day time, when he had more liberty. A glass of Hennessy's " Three Star " from the Hospital stores soon loosened his tongue, when he was handed over to one of our refugees who spoke Dutch, and the number of questions he had to answer was appalling. He told us many things that turned out true afterwards ; and, amongst others, of the intended attack on the Fort, which took place two days afterwards. The man could have had no reason for coming to us unless he was paid by the enemy for doing so, and was I suppose passed by their sentries as we were very closely invested—the tobacco was intended to soften our hearts. He also brought me, as an offering, a spoonful of salt in a paper.

Well on the morning of the 10th March, as our spy had foretold, the enemy commenced a general attack on our position, which lasted until sunset. Their gun, which was placed 700 yards from our rear face, was well protected by sand bags and bales of wood, and supported by the fire of about seventy rifles in shelter pits on each side of it.

The gun fired on this day eighty-three rounds, of which about forty struck our small work, scattering things in all directions and making matters generally unpleasant.

We placed the ladies in the Commissariat Marquee, the floor of which was deeply dug out on one side, and there they remained until the turmoil was over. Our men amused themselves for a long time by signalling to the enemy the shots of their gun, for the want of something better to do; but the fire that they drew caused this amusement to be stopped, much to their disappointment. I don't know what the enemy could have thought of this frolic; but to tell the truth situated as we were anything in the shape of amusement was welcome.

One would have thought there was now no ammunition left; but next morning the attack was renewed, with more men supporting the gun, and on this day it fired forty-seven rounds, of which about twenty-five struck the Fort. The rifle fire this day, was very trying, coming as it did by volleys from all four sides at uncertain intervals, not to speak of dropping fire going on all day from the trenches. These volleys must have been regulated in some way by signal, as the enemy themselves would have suffered. The wonder is that it did not wind up by a rush on our position. Our casualties on these two days were not heavy when the tremendous fire is considered.

Towards evening, when we thought the day's work was over, we sat down to dinner in our usual mess place. Hardly had we sat down when a round shot came in amongst us and covered the party with earth. For a few minutes we thought, "now they are coming," and the men went to their places.

We soon sat down again, thinking this was the last for

the night; and, having finished dinner, I got up and was standing near. We had been sitting on a bank of earth, with our backs to a wall of sand bags, and a lady of our party was on each side of me. Well, I had left the place a few seconds, when a round shot came and knocked away the sand bags just where my head had been, and missing the two ladies by less than a foot; this was the last for the night.

We made it very unpleasant for the enemy going home, just by way of saying good-night.

On the 17th March, finding things coming to a crisis, I determined to send our spy into the town, and offered him £100 to go there and bring me the latest news. He got there, no one can tell how, and at daybreak the next morning, the 18th of March, there was somewhat to our surprise, a pockethandkerchief flying on the top of his house—the preconcerted signal given by his wife to let us know of his arrival. One thing is to be remembered, and that is that the grass was very high and it was by no means impossible to creep through the Boer sentries as we had proved on former occasions. His house was on the outskirts of the town within view, and he pointed it out to us before leaving. That night he returned, and the news he gave us made it clear that the game was up. We had a consultation at once, and there was but one opinion as to the line to be taken. We had nothing more to eat, and our sick were dying from want of nourishment. Late that night I wrote a letter to the Boer commander proposing a meeting, and sent it off at sunrise next morning, the 19th, by a flag of truce. After some delay and a couple of letters on both sides, a meeting was arranged to take place at noon. Some time before the hour appointed up went a white flag, and we hoisted another in return.

Presently some mounted men appeared (for a Boer rarely walks), and along with them a Scotch cart. We watched this latter being unloaded, and spied amongst the contents a hamper. What feelings did not that hamper give rise to? I know some of us had visions of "French," as they call all but Cape brandy in these parts; and perhaps the thoughts of others might have been directed to "Square face," as they call Hollands Gin. As it turned out afterwards both of these were present, as were also biscuits and cigars. Our servants had been polishing up in an astonishing manner all the morning, and we marvelled at each other's appearance as we mustered to confront our antagonists at the water-furrow where the tent for the interview was pitched. I know I gave a considerable sum for a doubtful pair of "Peel's patent" to wear at that meeting. We turned out in a way that would have done no discredit to St. James's Street; even cigarettes were not wanting, our spy having brought us some the night before. One man said to me, "How are you all so clean when you come out of that hole?"

Well we sauntered down at the time appointed with the most nonchalant air, in order the better to conceal the true state of affairs.

A colonial marquee had been pitched at the water-furrow, 130 yards from the Fort, and there we shook hands for the first time with the men who shortly before had been trying all they knew to assist us into a better world. They certainly looked as if they had been having worse times than we had, to say the least of it. After preliminaries outside, we entered the tent, and settled down to business. A cigar and a glass of "French" now took the place of the cigarette, and the conference began. They contented themselves by saying "No" to everything we advanced, and to make headway under these these conditions was not easy.

They handed us an agreement ready for signature. By the terms of this, the Officers were to be free, and to keep their weapons and private property—this, it was expressly stated, was in consideration of the way we had fought our position, and our treatment of the Boer wounded. All the rest, "horse, foot, and artillery," and civilians, were to be prisoners of war; and everything in the Fort to be surrendered to the Transvaal Republic. The men knew that they had us in their power, they knew that we were very close to starvation, and they thought they had only to dictate terms for us to accept. They were wrong in this, however, for we really dictated terms to them next day—insomuch as we got many things that at first they refused to listen to. They would have given a good deal for the ammunition of the two nine pounder guns, but they did not get it notwithstanding. Seeing something desperate must be done I got up and announced my intention of going back to the Fort, and we all left the tent. After having gone a short distance, the Hollander interpreter came running after us, and said, "General Cronjé wished us to come back again." This I refused to do, but said if General Cronjé will come himself and give sufficient reason, then we might go back.

Cronjé came out and we went back. I gave them no time to say much as all was so unsatisfactory; so at once got up and gave my ultimatum, *viz*, that I would hold out to the last extremity, then send notice to send away all non-combatants, when I would fire three hundred shell into the town (burning it if possible) and two hundred thousand rounds of ammunition (neither of which I had) and then I would surrender. We then went away, but not before agreeing to meet next day at noon—to give time perhaps to consider the question of the conflagration.

Next day we met again, this time with the addition of the President of the Voolkraad, I taking another officer to balance numbers; and finally, after a tremendous palaver, came to an agreement. By the provisions of this, we were to march out with the honours of war and our flag flying, officers to retain their arms and private property, and none of us to be prisoners of war. The private property of the soldiers also to be kept by them.

They tried hard to make us give up our thirty-three civilians, including our spy, who would probably have been shot as a preliminary; but they reckoned without their host, and we took them all into Natal, except the Forssman family who made their temporary home in the Free State.

We kept all ammunition for field guns and rifles, but surrendered the two nine-pounders and the rifles, and the miscellaneous property in the Camp. The field guns and rifles were afterwards given up when the capitulation was cancelled. On the 21st of March we met again and signed the Treaty. So ended the "battle of words," much to our advantage under the circumstances, I think most people will say.

It may not be out of place here to relate, as shortly as I can, the story of the armistice entered into by General Sir Evelyn Wood and Piet Joubert at Mount Prospect, on the 6th March, 1881. The armistice was to extend from the 6th March at noon until midnight the 14th of March, 1881. The cause of the armistice was to give

Mr. Kruger time to consider and reply to the proposals made by the late Sir George Colley, and all further proposals which might be entertained between the respective parties with a view to settling the different disagreements.

ARTICLE 2 of the agreement of armistice provided that Sir Evelyn Wood was at liberty to send provisions and firewood, with the exception of ammunition, for eight days through the Boer lines to all his Garrisons in the Transvaal.

The Boer officials engaged to send on such provisions to the Garrisons, and the British Garrisons were to discontinue hostilities during eight days after the arrival of the provisions.

ARTICLE 3, provided that Piet Joubert was to make known this agreement of armistice at once to the Garrisons, and to the Boer Commanders at such places, &c.

On the 6th of March Sir Evelyn Wood, from Mount Prospect, wrote to President Brand, at Bloemfontein, acquainting his Honour of the agreement of armistice, and asking that the Boer Commander and the Officer in Command of the British Troops at Potchefstroom be informed, and made to understand that there is no armistice until the provisions have reached the Garrisons.

This President Brand faithfully carried out, and on the 12th of March Messrs. Mollett and Slnymers arrived at Potchefstroom, bringing a letter from the President to General Cronjé, and one to myself, as Commander of the Fort. This letter Cronjé refused to deliver, and on the 15th of March the Free State deputation left Potchefstroom, having exhausted their endeavours to get the letter delivered at the Fort.

On Wednesday, the 16th of March the *Staats Courant* published the agreement of Armistice ; but this also Cronjé witheld from me.

On the night of the 18th of March I learned some of the above from my spy who was sent by me into the town the day before, and this caused me to write the same night to the Boer commander, which resulted in the meeting which took place the next morning.

In accordance with Article 2 of the Agreement the late Captain Anton of the 94th Regiment, left Mount Prospect on the 6th or 7th of March with provisions for Standerton and Potchefstroom (taking also with him the draft of the agreement) and reached Standerton on the 12th but could

PART OF INTERIOR OF THE FORT, GAOL IN THE DISTANCE.

not cross the Drift as the river was in flood. He then went on to Standerton Old Drift and did not succeed in crossing the river until about the 26th, on which day I was crossing the Vaal on my way from Potchefstroom to Natal.

On the 16th Captain Mends of the 60th Rifles was sent from Mount Prospect with a letter prolonging the armistice to the 18th (four days), and with four days provisions for Standerton and Potchefstroom, reaching the former place on the 23rd. He found the river in flood and ultimately crossed it at a Drift some miles off on the 26th. While on the Vaal River on the 20th, he heard that Potchefstroom had fallen ; but could get nothing certain until the 30th, when he was at Zulkerbosh Rant River. He then returned to Heidelberg.

After signing the treaty at Potchefsroom the scene changed. All became *couleur de rose*. We went down the town and looked curiously at the Gaol, Landroost's Office, and other positions, and were well received by the inhabitants. Bullets had reached them and shells had missed their mark and fallen in their midst ; but they knew we had spared the town and the people in it as much as was possible. Introductions went on all day—there was the Commandant of Shuinspruit, the Commandant of Mooi River, the "Fighting General," and many others. Why this last was so named we don't know to this hour.

The Commandant of the Gun pressed forward for an introduction, and we complimented him on his practice, at which he seemed much pleased. One man was presented to us as "one of our bravest men ;" and if bravery consisted in stopping bullets he was rightly named, for he had his arm in a sling, one eye covered with a bandage and a third wound somewhere else. We were invited to breakfasts, luncheons, dinners, and consumed a quantity of "Dry Monopole" champagne that was surprising. An invitation to dine at the Royal Hotel with General Cronjé and his officers, was accepted. Five of us went to the dinner and were most hospitably entertained. It was a strange scene and not easily to be forgotten. There were about thirty at table, rough, hearty, determined looking men, of a class to command respect. I speak of the Boers, not of the Hollanders, who are not good advisers, and on whom they are too dependent.

The room was a large one, lined about three deep

round the walls by Boers with rifles, and as many as could see in through the windows were there also. We had an excellent dinner; and went there with the intention of enjoying ourselves, which in truth I believe we all did in spite of little drawbacks. Our doctor had spoken words of wisdom, counselling moderation, &c., overflowing with sage advice, but none of this did he follow himself when the time for action came. Many speeches (in Dutch, translated by a Hollander present) of a pleasant hearty character were made, and to all these a reply had to be given, taking up a good deal of time. Very full of good feeling were these speeches, and genuine I fully believe were the sentiments expressed.

But the beginning of the end was nearly reached when the Boer commander, carried away by his emotion, wound up in the speech of the evening by proposing to drink success to the Boer arms. I let him have his sweet will, and he resumed his seat amidst tumultous applause, banging of rifles on the floor and shouting in the street. This sentiment was rather overpowering however, even allowing the "dry Monopole" its due weight, and I saw with alarm the moustache of one of my young Scotch subalterns positively bristling. I felt thankful that his sword and revolver were in the next room. He looked positive daggers at me, as if I was the real culprit, and I felt that it was do or die with me.

The oration over, I rose and, after replying to the first part of the speech, told my hearers that the sentiment in the latter part was of a nature that I could not respond to. Anything less like satisfaction at the efforts of an orator it has not been my fate so see; so, thinking to divert the current of their thoughts, I promptly proposed the health of General Cronjé and his Officers, who had lately been our enemies, but were now our friends. Happily this had the desired effect, and there was some applause and hammering of rifles on the floor.

Good feeling culminated when General Cronjé gave me his hand across the table, and we drank the toast amidst great excitement from those at the table and the mob outside, who seemed fully aware of all that was going on.

Our nerves were at this time pretty highly strung, and we were ready for any new adventure, so I was not surprised at feeling my shoulder touched by a friendly waiter. I put down my hand instinctively, and into it dropped a note, which I read under the table. This warned me to be careful, as some of the mob outside had determined to shoot me on my way home. This was pleasing news to receve at a festive gathering, and I only hoped that the bullet would miss me and hit——well, somebody else.

After leaving the table, and while in the passage, which was densely crowded, a similar warning was conveyed to me. I said nothing of this to any of my officers, but kept my ears open, and what I heard convinced me of the good faith of our entertainers. I saw General Cronjé assemble his officers, and, knowing a few words of Dutch, I could make out sufficient to know that he was in the most solemn mannor charging them with our safety. I found a buggy waiting to take me home, two of the chief Boer leaders got in and I was invited to sit between them, and two more got up behind; so all was done that was possible, and my officers were treated in the same kindly fashion.

When we got outside it was pitch dark, and we passed through a dense crowd at a walk, escorted to the Fort by the Boers, and, on arrival there, took leave of them in the most cordial manner.

The whole affair was characterised by genuine good feeling, our entertainers doing their utmost to make us feel at home, and I must say they succeeded in this. All our dealings after the capitulation went smoothly and the Boers seemed anxious that this should be so.

It was arranged that we shonld evacuate our position and march from Potchefstroom on the 23rd of March. The night before we packed our waggons, and early on the morning of the 23rd fell in on the glacis and marched down to the water-furrow, our flag at our head and the buglers playing a march.

There we found the Boers drawn up, a fine soldierly lot of men, in number about four hundred. Previous to marching off Cronjé came up to me, and with him a Burgher holding a horse, which I was invited to ride. The horses we had bought the day before stood ready saddled in the ditch. I mounted the horse sent by the Boer General; and my officers mounted the one held by their groom, which most of them saw for the first time, they having had no time to make choice of animals. There was scarcely a saddle in the lot that had not a bullet through it, and some had several. At the water-furrow we opened our ranks and laid down our arms, and soon after marched off with part of the Boers as advanced guard and the remainder behind. They escorted us through the town and about a mile beyond.

Then Cronjé made a farewell speech, and his leading men crowded round to grasp our hands and wish us God speed, no doubt as glad as ourselves that fighting was over. This done, they formed up on each side of the road, and saluted us as we marched through their ranks—no troops in any part of the world could have taken more polite farewell, or behaved more courteously throughout.*

Every man, woman, and child was with us in marching from Potchefstroom, except two badly wounded men whom we were forced to leave to the care of the doctors in town.

We continued our march to Vyf Hoek, the farm of Captain Baillie, late of the 7th Hussars, where a halt had been arranged, in order to make our arrangements for a march through the Orange Free State into Natal.

All next day we halted there, and met with nothing but kindness from every one; one Dutchman sending fifty ducks for our Hospital, in which we had twenty-three patients, fifteen of these being wounded.

The day before leaving I rode with one of my officers into the town and visited one of the Stores to get some things for the march, including some underclothing, which we were much in want of. These things could not be sold, the proprietor said; the Boers would not permit it, or something of the sort. We did not understand this and could get nothing more out of the man, so in the end we had to go away without getting what we wanted. On relating this to our kind host, for we were all living in his house, he led us into a room and there we found everything we had ordered, and many things besides, in paper, ready to be packed to go into

---

* The capitulation, it may be remembered, was afterwards cancelled, and Potchefstroom re-occupied by our troops for a short time.

This cancelling was proposed by the Boer triumvirate in consequence of the action taken by Cronjé in withholding from the garrison, contrary to his orders, the terms of the agreement entered into by Sir Evelyn Wood and Piet Joubert on the 6th March, 1881.

Had Cronjé fulfilled his instructions, affairs would have turned out differently, and the capitulation would not have taken place.

our waggon. His house was turned into a store, but all the things were gifts, freely distributed to all all of us. The sick, too, were not forgotten, and I don't believe a soldier went away empty handed.

One sad duty remained to us before quitting Vyf Hoek, and that was the placing in consecrated ground the remains of our brother officer who fell at the Landroost's Office on the 16th of December. A kind friend, the Manager of the Standard Bank, had taken the body and buried it in his garden, as the Cemetery was not available at the time on account of its position within our lines. The coffin was disinterred by our men and placed in the Cemetery, all officers off duty attending to perform this last service to a departed comrade.

We had also to bury our two men who had been left behind the day before, for they, poor fellows, lived only long enough to hear our bugles play us through the town. I don't believe there was a man of our party who did not think of these two, as we marched past the hospital where they lay, and wish that we had them with us.

Before leaving we did all that was possible to the graves of our soldiers who had fallen during the siege, and this work, I am told, was completed by the Garrison that went there later. The casualties during the siege were as follows, viz. :—

Killed in action, or died of wounds	25
Died of disease	6
Wounded	54
Total	85

This includes eight civilians.

When taken into consideration the continued fire day and night for ninety-five days of the most searching and accurate character, and every bullet directed into a small space of 25 yards square, filled with people, the marvel is that the loss was not greater.

The casualties in detail were as under :—

Nature of Casualties.	Officers.	N.C. Officers	Soldiers.	Civilians.	Women.	Children.	Total.
Killed & died of wounds	1	2	19	2	—	1	25
Died of disease	—	1	3	—	1	1	6
Wounded	5	6	40	2	—	1	54
Total	6	9	62	4	1	3	85

The above is taken from the official returns, but a good many slight wounds are not included in the return. For instance, the girl who was wounded in the neck is not included.

Of the above, one man was wounded three times, and four men were wounded twice—counting five in the return instead of eleven. It is no exaggeration to say that the bullet holes in our six tents numbered several thousands, besides a few round shot. All the hospital tents were completely riddled: and even in the tent, where the lady was dying, a round shot struck the pole and covered her with splinters.

To give some idea of the gun and rifle fire on one day, I may mention that on the 10th of March the enemy had about seventy men guarding their gun. In the interval of loading nearly every one of these discharged his rifle with the object of keeping down our fire. The gun fired eighty-three rounds on this day, and therefore 5,810 rounds (70 × 83) might be estimated to have come from around the gun alone. Besides this, a heavy fire was kept up the whole day from the trenches; and a number of volleys were fired from all four sides at certain intervals from sunrise to sunset.

Of the Boer casualties during the siege it is difficult to form any estimate. Fifteen burials are known to have taken place on one day—this we had from the best authority, and is all we know for certainty. The Boer leaders in Potchefstroom, as in other places, were careful to conceal their losses; and until they dispersed to their homes, the Boers themselves did not know their true loss.

Early on the morning of the 25th of March we left our generous host, and set off on our march to Natal, through the Orange Free State, that way being likely to prove more agreeable than through the Transvaal. On the 26th we arrived at De Wet's Drift on the Vaal, and spent that day and part of the next in crossing the river by the "pont" or floating bridge. On the opposite bank, in the Free State Territory, we halted for two days enjoying ourselves thoroughly. No more firing or sitting up at night! Nothing but profound repose! We felt like birds let out of a cage, free as the air we lived in. We were entirely in the open, but to that we were accustomed, and rather liked it in such a climate.

Our men made shelters with their blankets, and we officers did the same. The men spent most of the day in the river, washing their clothes and enjoying themselves generally. Letter writing under a tree took up a good deal of time at the first, and I wrote my report for despatch to Head Quarters.

On the 29th we again marched, and arrived at Cronstadt on the 4th of April. Here we handed our gun and small arm ammunition to the care of the authorities—as provided for in the Treaty made at Potchefstroom—to be returned to the British Government at the close of the war.

We bivouacked by the river bank among the trees, and received visits without number, and invitations to entertainments of all sorts. The Union Jack was displayed all over the town on our arrival, and the people did all in their power to make our stay a pleasant one. One Dutchman hoisted the flag of the Transvaal Republic; but as we got into the town it was hauled down; some of the people saying we would not like it. A man took the trouble to ride out and tell me this. We were entertained at dinner on the day of arrival by some hospitable Englishman, and I must say we spent a very noisy evening. A Cricket Match was played, which occasioned great excitement, spectators coming from far and near.

On the 11th of April we left Cronstadt on our way to Harrismith. On this day we took leave of the Consul-General for Portugal (the Chevalier Forssman) and his family. They drove a long way with us on our march, and we shook hands for the last time with the members of this family, with whom we had been so closely associated. Few ladies have had a rougher experience or gone through one more bravely. We were truly sorry to part ; but our roads lay in different directions, so we said "Good-bye," wondering if we should ever meet again.

We arrived at Harrismith on the 24th of April, and remained there three days, resting our sick, and making preparations for a fresh start. A ball was got up for us, and we danced until four o'clock in the morning ; and at eight o'clock most of us were present at a wedding at the English Church, a pretty little edifice on the outskirts of the town. Two hours after this marched and crossed the Drakensberg Range into Natal by Van Renan's Pass, 6,000 feet above sea level, on the 30th of April. On the 2nd of May, 1881, we arrived at Ladysmith, having completed our journey all well, and with sick and wounded much improved by the march. Here we found tents waiting for us, a luxury we had not known for nearly five months.

The Officers of the Garrison were as follows :—

Commanding Officer—Major and Brevet Lieut.-Colonel R. W. C. Winsloe, 2nd Batt. Royal Scots Fusiliers.

Officer Commanding R.A.—Major C. Thornhill, Royal Artillery.

Commissariat Officer—D.A.C.G. W. A. Dunne.

The other Officers were :—

Capt. A. L. Falls, 2nd Batt. Royal Scots Fusiliers (killed).

Lieut. H. L. M. Rundle, Royal Artillery.

,, P. W. Browne, 2nd Batt. Royal Scots Fusiliers.
,, C. F. Lindsell, ,, ,, ,, ,, ,,
,, K. E. Lean, ,, ,, ,, ,, ,,
,, Dalrymple Hay ,, ,, ,, ,, ,,

Brevet-Major M. J. Clarke, Royal Artillery, was in Potchefstroom-town as Special Commissioner ; and on the death of Captain Falls, at the Landroost's Office, was the only officer left there.

PART OF THE INTERIOR OF THE FORT, MAGAZINE IN THE DISTANCE.

DETAIL OF GARRISON.

Corps.	Officers.	Non-Com. Officers and Men.	Total.
Royal Artillery	2	43	45
Royal Scots Fusiliers	4	125	129
Mounted Infantry }			
Royal Scots Fusiliers {	2	24	26
Commissariat	1	7	8
Medical Department	1	4	5
Total	10	203	213

REFUGEES.

Men.	Women.	Children.	Total.	
13	19	16	48	Eight men, 13 women, 16 children left during the siege.

TRANSPORT.

Conductor.	Caffre Drivers and Leaders.	Total.	
1	60	61	39 Drivers and Leaders left during the siege.

SUMMARY.

Officers, Non-Com. Officers, and Men.	Refugees.	Transport.	Total.
213	48	61	322

ANIMALS.

Horses.	Mules.	Oxen.	Total.
76	121	147	344

All these, except one horse, had to be turned adrift on on the sixth day of the investment.

WAGGONS.

Mule and Ox Waggons,	Ambulance Waggons	Water Carts.	Ammunition Carts	Total
17	2	3	2	24

In justice to the little Garrison I had the honour of commanding, I subjoin a copy of a District Order, issued by the Officer Commanding in the Transvaal, and with this I close what is at least a faithful account of events that will not soon pass from the memory of those who participated in them.

DISTRICT ORDER.

"PRETORIA,

7th April, 1881.

The Fort at Potchefstroom capitulated on the 21st March, but only when its garrison was reduced to extremity, and after as brave a defence as any in military annals; the troops marching out with the honours of war, and proceeding through the Orange Free State to Natal. The sterling qualities, for which British soldiers have been renowned, have been brilliantly shown in this instance, during a long period of privation under very trying circumstances.

Colonel Bellairs begs Lieut.-Colonel Winsloe, and the Officers and men under him, will accept his thanks for the proud and determined way in which they have performed their duty.

By Order,

(Signed) M. CHURCHILL, Captain, D.A.A.G."

www.ingramcontent.com/pod-product-compliance
Lightning Source LLC
Chambersburg PA
CBHW051716040426
42446CB00008B/915